Museum in Docklands

Highlights

Chris Ellmers

MUSEUM
IN DOCKLANDS

© Museum in Docklands, 2003

First published in 2003
by the Museum of London

All photographs © Museum of London
unless otherwise stated

ISBN 0 904 818 52 7

Edited by Dr Anita Phillips
Designed by Vermillion
and the Museum of London

Printed and bound in 2003
by Colorman Ltd

Front cover photograph
Dockers trucking heavy bags of sugar
at 'Blood Alley', on the North Quay of
the West India Docks, around 1930

Back cover photograph
The entrance to the Museum
in Docklands

Grateful thanks to Torla Evans,
John Chase and Richard Stroud, for
photography; Dr Tom Wareham, Paul
More and Alison Guppy, for the
preparation of objects; Andy Topping,
Dr Tom Wareham, Oriel Williams and
Alex Werner for helpful advice and
selected text contributions.

Contents

Foreword

The Museum in Docklands grew out of an important collecting and recording initiative begun by the Museum of London in 1979. At that time, the last of the upriver docks and many of the riverside wharves and factories were facing closure. 1982 saw publication of the first formal proposals for a museum in Docklands to present the little-known story of London's river and port and the people living and working there. It was envisaged as a major cultural focus for the East London region, a place which would generate and reinforce a sense of pride for communities old and new.

A magnificent but run-down late Georgian warehouse at the West India Docks was chosen from the start as the ideal building. Thanks both to the dogged determination of the Museum of London team and generous support from the London Docklands Development Corporation, the Heritage Lottery Fund and other stakeholders, the Museum in Docklands finally opened there in May 2003. It had been a long and difficult, but worthwhile journey.

In 1929, John Burns, the veteran Labour politician, 1889 dock strike leader, and London writer and guide, coined the phrase: 'The River Thames is Liquid History.' Burns had great insight. Without the river, London would not have existed. The river has made London the great international centre of business that it is today, and one of the world's most vibrant and cosmopolitan cities. For two thousand years, the river has been a two-way route for people, trade and ideas. All of these are part of the Museum's story – a fascinating mix of the local, the national and the international.

Chris Ellmers

This guidebook presents some of the highlights of the Museum in Docklands. A range of objects, from humble dockers' hooks to splendid models and fine paintings, together with gallery reconstructions, evoke elements of the two-thousand-year story of *London's river, port and people*.

The introductions to each gallery section will help the reader navigate some of the key moments of the story. Individual descriptions of selected objects, images and reconstructions help flesh it out. But no souvenir guide can convey the feel, sounds and smells of the galleries. To enjoy these – and the exhibits not included here – we hope that the reader will return for further visits.

As only part of the Museum's extensive collection is on display, and as many subjects are worthy of greater attention, there are supporting programmes of special events, exhibitions and publications.

The Museum in Docklands is one of three sites run by the Museum of London. Mortimer Wheeler House in Hackney, East London, houses the London Archaeological Archive and Research Centre where the finds from over 5000 archaeological digs are deposited and can be examined. The Museum of London based in the City tells the story of London from prehistoric times to the early twentieth century. More information on our sites can be found at www.museumoflondon.org.uk

'And for a continuous and living picture of English life, there is no river better than the Thames.'
F V Morley

The Building

The Museum occupies three of the five bays of No. 1 Warehouse, West India Quay. The West India Docks, opened in 1802, were London's first purpose-built cargo handling docks. No. 1 Warehouse was one of the nine linked warehouses designed by the architects, George Gwilt and his son, also named George. The warehouses stretched for more than a kilometre along the north side of the Import Dock. Benefiting from the docks' twenty-one-year monopoly, they stored vast quantities of rum, sugar, molasses, coffee, pimento and cotton from West India slave plantations.

No. 1 Warehouse was originally built, between 1802 and 1804, as a one- and two-storey building over basements. It was heightened in 1827 to attract the East India tea trade. New London stock bricks, distinctive cast-iron spiked windows, and pitch pine timbers harmonised with those of the earlier structure. The westernmost bay housed ships' bonded stores in the basement, and functioned until 1834 as a baggage warehouse above. From 1834 to 1883, the building was one of London's largest tea warehouses, receiving cargoes from clipper ships. After that the building stored canned fish, dried fruit, sugar, molasses, shells, canes, steel and timber board.

The building survived a fire in 1901 and enemy bombing during the Second World War. Of the original warehouses, only No. 1 Warehouse and the adjoining No. 2 Warehouse escaped the Blitz of September 1940. The warehouses closed in 1968 and were converted between 1999 and 2003. Now Grade 1 Listed, they are the sole surviving major Georgian dock warehouses in any British seaport.

The Westernmost bay of the Museum building, around 1920

River, Port and People

The galleries of the Museum in Docklands trace the fascinating two-thousand-year story of London's river, port and people. It is a story that stretches from the arrival of the Romans to the rise of Canary Wharf. In this introductory gallery, TV personality Tony Robinson outlines the importance of the Thames to London throughout history. Taking his view from the historic City foreshore and the Canary Wharf Tower, Tony Robinson emphasises the role of the river in facilitating the movement of people and the development of trade. Without the river, there would be no London.

The centrepiece of the gallery is a waterman's skiff, set against a reconstructed quayside. The skiff – appropriately called the *Thames* – was built at Gravesend, by Warner, in 1935. Traditionally, watermen's skiffs were used to carry passengers and river workers. They originated from eighteenth century Thames' 'bumboats,' which ferried ships' supplies and provisions. The Eagleton and Gobbett families of Blackwall watermen used the *Thames*. As well as being lightermen, or barge owners, the Gobbetts also acted as general watermen and 'dock pilots' at the West India Docks. The *Thames* was used to assist ships entering and berthing in the docks until 1978.

The walls and floors of the gallery are dramatically used to project moving words and acronyms. Some of these may appear strange to visitors. By the time that the Museum journey is complete, their meanings should have become clear. As Tony Robinson says, it is now time for the visitor to 'dig deep' and 'peel back the layers of history.'

Tony Robinson introduces the gallery video

Thames Highway
AD50–1600

The story begins around AD50, with the Roman settlement in what is now the City of London. As early as AD61, Tacitus described London as 'an important centre for merchants'. Luxury and utilitarian cargoes came from across the Roman Empire. London exported grain, hides, metals and slaves.

The Roman troops withdrew in AD410. The Anglo-Saxon settlers avoided the old Roman walled city. By AD600, the Saxon settlement of 'Lundenwic' was well established, with a beach market along the line of the present day Aldwych and the Strand. Bede described it as 'the mart of many nations.' Attacked by Vikings, the Saxons abandoned the settlement in favour of the old walled city around AD886. New beach markets lined the waterfront of 'Lundenburgh' east and west of a timber bridge.

Between 1176 and 1209, the City built a massive new stone London Bridge. The waterfront was successively embanked between 1200 and 1500. In 1389 the City became responsible for managing the river, between Staines and the Medway, including its fish stocks. In 1559, twenty-one Legal Quays were established on the City waterfront, for the handling of all dutiable cargoes. After 1550, groups of merchant venturers reaped the combined benefits of protective trading monopolies, a stronger navy and declining European ports. In 1566, Thomas Gresham founded a meeting house for merchants in Cornhill. It became the Royal Exchange in 1571. By the 1590s, trade expansion had resulted in the rapid development of riverside communities east of the City.

Reconstructed view of the beach market of Lundenwic

Roman amphora

London imported many products from other parts of the Roman Empire. Amphora are large clay storage jars used for transporting wine, olive oil, olives, dried fruit and fish products. Amphora varied in size, the very largest being used for wine, which was imported from the Mediterranean as early as AD50 or 60. Amphora finds are numerous from the sites of Roman quaysides to the east of the Roman bridge.

This particular amphora is from Roman London. It once contained a popular fish sauce known as *garum*, produced around Cadiz in the southern Spanish region of Baetica. Fish sauce was also imported from Italy, Morocco and Brittany. About a fifth of all London amphora finds are of Spanish *garum* containers, indicating that this trade was very important. There is no archaeological evidence of Spanish fish sauce being imported after the end of the second century.

The spike at the base of the amphora acted as a third handle when lifting and pouring the contents.

Roman amphora, used for fish sauce, around AD100

Venetian glass

Fabrics, foodstuffs, woad, wine and metal products dominated imports during the Tudor period. Much was destined for London's wealthy inhabitants. Imported luxuries included musical instruments, weapons, tapestries, carpets, glass and ceramics.

The Venetians developed an important glass industry, whose exports dominated Europe from around 1400 to 1700. These fragments are part of a blue and gold enamelled glass vessel imported into London. In the late fifteenth century and at the beginning of the sixteenth,

Fragments of an imported enamelled blue Venetian glass vessel, around 1480–1500

Venetian glass workers could produce blue, green, purple and opaque white vessels. These were decorated and fired with coloured enamels. Goblets and chalices were often commissioned to celebrate marriages.

Medieval London Bridge model

Section of the model of the eastern side of London Bridge, around 1440

Around 1170, Peter de Colechurch, the Bridge Master and Chaplain of St Mary Colechurch, proposed the building of a new stone bridge to replace the wooden one. Wealthy Londoners provided funds for its construction, between 1176 and 1209. The bridge was a wonder of the medieval world and an engineering marvel. Nineteen ragstone arches rested on twenty piers, or 'starlings.' These starlings consisted of elmwood piles driven into the riverbed, filled with rubble and capped with oak sills. Sadly, de Colechurch died four years before the bridge's completion.

This model section is of the southern part of the eastern side, around 1440. On the left are the drawbridge and drawbridge gate, as rebuilt from 1427. The drawbridge, first mentioned in 1257, allowed shipping to reach Queenhithe. The drawbridge gate had a portcullis, to defend the City. The heads of executed traitors were displayed on the parapet of the bridge.

On the right of the group of buildings is the stone Chapel of St Thomas, which stood towards the centre of the bridge. The chapel was dedicated to Thomas à Becket, murdered in Canterbury Cathedral in 1170, and canonised in 1172. The building seen here replaced the original one between 1384 and 1397.

The chapel was a magnet for pilgrims on their way to and from Canterbury. King Henry VIII attempted to erase the memory of this popular saint: the building was defaced in 1539 and 1540, and converted to a dwelling in 1553.

In 1358 there were 128 shops, with living accommodation above, on the bridge. There were seventeen between the drawbridge and the chapel, on the eastern side. Of these, five had *hautepas* – top floors built across the street below. An army of workmen maintained the bridge. The cost of upkeep was met from property rentals and tolls for both bridge users and vessels passing beneath.

Trade Expansion
1600–1800

Developments in shipbuilding, seamanship and navigational knowledge helped the growth of Britain's overseas interests. Protected by an increasingly powerful navy, Britain challenged her European rivals for trade and territory. International expansion was mirrored in the growth of London, its population and its port activities.

The largest ships dominated trade with the East and West Indies, North America, the Baltic and the Mediterranean. Between 1600 and 1798, the number of coastal and overseas ships using London rose from 3000 to 14,600. The business of the port was transacted in City coffee houses, the Royal Exchange and merchants' 'counting houses.' The most valuable cargoes were handled at the Legal Quays, between London Bridge and the Tower. As port trade increased in the eighteenth century, HM Customs allowed 'Sufferance Wharves' on the Bermondsey and St Katharine's waterfronts. Only the smaller ships could discharge directly at these quays and wharves.

Larger ships – from coal-blackened Newcastle colliers to grand East Indiamen – were discharged into lighters below Wapping. Ropewalks, sail lofts, ship smiths, anchor smiths and nautical instrument makers were to be found at Wapping, Ratcliffe, Limehouse, Rotherhithe, Deptford, Blackwall and Woolwich.

Busy and culturally diverse riverside communities serviced ships and sailors. Housing was often overcrowded and insanitary, in contrast with the grand riverside houses west of Westminster Bridge (which opened in 1750). Many of these had been built from the profits of London's port and overseas trade.

The busy Pool of London in 1799

Pocahontas wooden figure

This fine carved and painted mid-eighteenth century wooden figure has long been known as *Pocahontas*. This links it with the Virginia Settlers, who sailed from Blackwall in 1606, to become the first permanent British settlers in North America. Pocahontas, daughter of the powerful Native American Alongonquian chief, Powhatan, became famous for saving the life of Captain John Smith. She married John Rolfe in 1614 and died in England – probably of smallpox – in 1616. Pocahontas was buried at Gravesend. The hard-pressed Virginia Settlers introduced tobacco in 1613. It quickly became a major cash crop, finding a ready market in London. By the 1660s, African slaves were being used to replace white indentured labourers to grow tobacco. Soon much of Virginia and Maryland, around the Chesapeake, were growing tobacco. In 1770 the two states had 250,000 slaves, and the tobacco they produced formed one of London's major trades.

As *Pocahontas* is shown wearing a head-dress and skirt of stylised tobacco leaves, this was probably a tobacconist shop's advertising figure. It is very similar to ships' figure-heads of the time. Shop figures were mostly made around Harp Alley, Shoe Lane, in the City of London, while ships' figurehead carvers were to be found in Wapping, Limehouse and Rotherhithe. Some carvers would have worked in both fields.

Carved wooden figure, *Pocahontas*, around 1750

Porters

Porters licensed by the City Corporation did most cargo handling. The Fellowship of Billingsgate Porters handled grain, malt, salt, fish, fruit, vegetables and other measurable cargoes. They wore brass licence badges attached to pierced leather tallies, on which different jobs could be recorded by cord thongs.

Ticket Porters handled cargoes from the West Indies, America, Canada, Ireland and coastal ports. They also handled other imported cargoes for the wealthy Tacklehouse Porters. 'Uptown' Ticket Porters carried packages and sacks to and from the Legal Quays. Ticket Porters

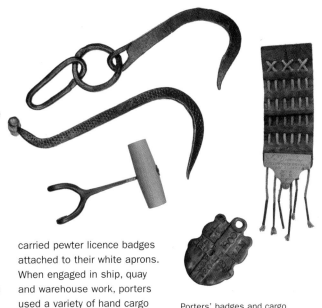

carried pewter licence badges attached to their white aprons. When engaged in ship, quay and warehouse work, porters used a variety of hand cargo hooks.

Porters' badges and cargo hooks, eighteenth-century

Octant

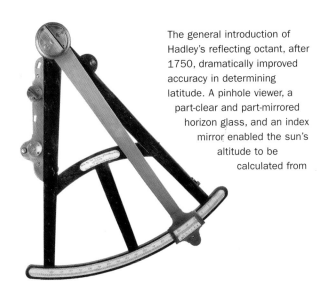

The general introduction of Hadley's reflecting octant, after 1750, dramatically improved accuracy in determining latitude. A pinhole viewer, a part-clear and part-mirrored horizon glass, and an index mirror enabled the sun's altitude to be calculated from the 95 degree divided arc. Used in conjunction with tables of lunar distances, octants could also be used to determine longitude at sea, by establishing the distance of certain stars from the moon.

The Wapping mathematical instrument maker, Thomas Ripley, made this mahogany, brass and ivory octant, with additional vernier scale. Ripley worked at the 'Sign of the Globe, Quadrant and Spectacles,' Hermitage Basin. The ivory plaque notes that it was made 'For Alexr. McLaren Sept 17.1770.'

Octant made by Thomas Ripley, 1770

The *Falmouth* East Indiaman

Shown here is the cut-away side of the Museum's splendid model of the East India Company's ship, the *Falmouth*. She was launched at John Perry's Blackwall Yard in August 1752. Trading to India and China, East Indiamen were the largest ships afloat. The *Falmouth's* keel measured thirty-three metres (109 feet) and she was 678 tonnes (669 tons) in weight. She was heavily armed with thirty guns and carried an official crew of ninety-nine. Of her six voyages, five were to India. The model shows her as she would have looked in 1764, returning from her only trip to China. The cut-away section reveals the huge

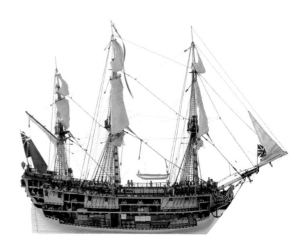

Model of the *Falmouth*, depicted in 1764

cargo of tea chests, bales of silk, cases of chinaware and bags of spices brought home by East Indiamen. She was wrecked in June 1766, near Bengal.

Gibbet cage

Iron gibbet cage, around 1750

During the eighteenth century, world trade routes were still terrorised by pirates who plundered shipping. Concerted efforts by the Royal Navy, Royal Africa Company and East India Company gradually reduced their numbers. Many captured pirates were brought to London for trial before the High Court of Admiralty. The conviction rate was high. Public executions were carried out at 'Execution Dock' on the Wapping foreshore, where temporary gallows were erected.

The corpses of the more notorious pirates were then tarred and hung on wooden gibbets in iron cages, or chains. The gruesome spectacle of their rotting bodies, exhibited along the riverbank, was seen as a great deterrent. The gibbeting of executed pirates continued into the nineteenth century. This wrought iron gibbet cage is from the mid-eighteenth century. The upper cage and collar are designed to unbolt and hinge open. The suspension eye shows signs of considerable wear.

Legal Quay

Part of the Legal Quay reconstruction, around 1790

This reconstruction brings together some of the different elements, activities and sounds of London's late eighteenth-century Legal Quays. A 'counting house' – then the name for an office – belonging to a wharfinger or wharf operator is set beneath a treadwheel crane. The crane is used to discharge and load cargoes. The busy waterfront by Billingsgate can be glimpsed beyond. Goods and cargo handling equipment, including a large beamscale – used to weigh cargoes – occupy the space between two warehouses. It is early morning and the Customs officers, sailors, merchants, wharfingers, ships' husbands, lumpers (stevedores), porters, lightermen, coopers, watchmen, carmen, fishwives and street sellers are getting ready for their day's work.

Overcrowding on the river, on the wharves and in the warehouses had become a serious problem by the 1790s. It caused expensive delays to shipowners and merchants, and an alarming level of theft and pilferage. As London's port trade continued to expand, so did these problems.

The Rhinebeck Panorama

The semi-circular Rhinebeck Panorama recreation provides a birds-eye view of the metropolis, seen from the east. Part of the central section is seen here. Although dated to between 1806 and 1811, the crowded shipping scene in the Upper Pool of London is essentially that of late 1790s, before the opening of the enclosed docks. Most of the ships depicted are European traders and British coasters. Shown here are the historic Legal Quays, below London Bridge, established in 1559 for the handling of all dutiable cargoes. On the Bermondsey waterfront are the Sufferance Wharves, established in the eighteenth century to relieve the crowded Legal Quays. Besides ships, the river is also busy with sailing barges, lighters, watermen's passenger-carrying wherries and ceremonial craft.

A 2.5 metre (eight foot) long watercolour in four sections, the Panorama was the work of three different artists. One provided the main features. The second drew the vessels and a third heightened the church towers and steeples. Given its size, viewpoint and remarkable detail, the picture was almost certainly the artwork for a much larger painted show panorama. Displayed in special buildings, panoramas and dioramas of cities and famous battles were popular forms of middle-class entertainment in Regency London.

The Panorama's early history is not known, but Robert Havell Junior updated and reproduced it as an engraving in 1831. In 1839, Havell emigrated to the United States, settling in the Hudson Valley, New York State. The Panorama was rediscovered there, in the loft of a house in Rhinebeck, in 1941. It was acquired by the Museum of London in 1998.

Part of the City section of the Rhinebeck Panorama

The Coming of the Docks

1800–1820

London's coastal and overseas trade trebled in tonnage during the eighteenth century. By the 1790s the annual value of overseas trade had reached £50 million, and coastal trade £11 million. Although trade had expanded, port facilities had not. Overcrowding, congestion, delays and theft threatened the port's future. Port reformers campaigned for better policing and the building of enclosed trading docks. London already had two large enclosed docks – the Greenland Dock, at Rotherhithe (opened in 1699) – and the Brunswick Dock, at Blackwall (opened 1789). Built for re-fitting and laying-up ships, their trading operations were highly restricted.

The magistrate Patrick Colquhoun reckoned that a quarter of all port workers were corrupt, costing merchants and HM Customs half a million pounds a year in lost income. Colquhoun's Marine Police Establishment came into being in 1798 to police the river and the quays.

Parliament finally passed Acts for the building of new trading docks east of the Tower. The West India Docks, which cut across the north of the Isle of Dogs, opened in 1802 and the London Docks, at Wapping, in 1805. In 1806 the East India Docks opened at Blackwall. Between them, they enjoyed specific twenty-one year monopolies on most dutiable cargoes. The Legal Quays and Sufferance Wharves lost their privileges. The City Canal opened in 1805 to the south of the West India Docks. In Rotherhithe, new timber and grain handling docks were developed around the Greenland Dock. By 1810, London had the best port facilities in the world.

Detail of Brunswick Dock, Blackwall, in 1803, by William Daniell

The London Docks

William Daniell's view of the projected London Docks, 1803

Between 1802 and 1813, William Daniell published a series of six large hand-coloured aquatints of London's new docks. The prints are of the West India Docks (1802); two of the London Docks (1803 and 1808); Brunswick Dock (1803); East India Docks (1805) and the Commercial Docks (1813). They are the only contemporary views to properly convey the extent and impact of the new docks.

Daniell's 1803 print of the London Docks was dedicated to its Chairman and Directors. It was published two years before the dock opened to shipping. Confronted with an unfinished dock, Daniell would have made use of John Fairburn's 1802 plan and Daniel Asher Alexander's architectural drawings of the proposed buildings. The result was a remarkably accurate picture. Daniell's prints cost two pounds, twelve shillings and sixpence each – more than three weeks' average wages for dock labourers.

Dock labourer's badge

The West India Dock Company issued this brass licence badge, between 1802 and 1810, to one of its permanent labourers at the North Quay Warehouses. The early dock companies distinguished between permanent labourers and casual men. In August 1805 – a busy time at the West India Docks – the number of labourers employed at the North Quay Warehouses varied from around 900 to about 1300. Only 300 to 350 of these were permanent.

Fully employed dock labourers earned one pound a week. The

Labourer's badge, from the West India Docks, around 1802–1810

West India Dock Company forced its labourers to buy 'strong and useful working frocks, uniformly made and marked, and numbered so as to identify the wearer.' By 1821, some extra labourers only worked for an hour at a time. Thomas Farnsworth, a representative of striking West India Dock coopers, said that the hiring of labourers was a 'a disgrace to the slave-markets in the West Indies.'

George Hibbert

A leading port reformer, George Hibbert (1757–1837) had initially backed William Vaughan's Wapping Dock scheme in 1793. He was, however, soon supporting Robert Milligan's rival proposal for a separate dock on the Isle of Dogs for the West India trade. Hibbert was well placed to become the major player in the West India Docks. A leading West India merchant since the early 1780s, Hibbert also owned ships and had plantation interests. Hibbert operated Wiggins Quay, one of the Legal Quays. He was a City Common Councillor, becoming an Alderman in 1798. He was instrumental in gaining the City Corporation's support for the West India Docks proposal, which received Royal Assent in 1799.

Hibbert was elected one of the City Aldermanic Directors of the West India Dock Company at its inaugural meeting in August 1799. He then became its first Chairman, a position he held until 1801, and again in 1803 to 1804 and 1815. Politically, Hibbert was a staunch Whig and friend of William Pitt, the Prime Minister, who officiated at the laying of the docks' foundation stone in July 1800. Hibbert represented Seaford as MP between 1806 and 1812. His position as the most important West India merchant was strengthened when he became chairman of the powerful West India Committee

George Hibbert by Sir Thomas Lawrence, 1811

and the Agent for Jamaica.

Despite his strong personal and business association with slavery, Hibbert was widely regarded as a liberal patron of the arts. A Fellow of the Royal Society, founder member of the London Institution, and editor of Ovid's *Metamorphoses*, Hibbert collected books and paintings.

The sale of his library in 1829 took forty-two days. In 1811, a grateful West India Dock Company commissioned Sir Thomas Lawrence to paint his portrait, at a cost of 300 guineas. Hibbert's hand rests on a plan of the West India Docks and part of the vast Import Dock is seen behind.

City and River
1820–1840

The period 1820 to 1840 was a watershed, characterised by powerful economic, technological and social change. The end of the dock companies' twenty-one year monopolies, together with pressure for free trade, heralded a period of destructive competition. St Katharine Docks opened as London's first purpose-built free trade dock in 1828. The forced clearance of the urban site, east of the Tower, raised social issues that were to echo through time to the Docklands' redevelopment of the 1980s.

The opening of John Rennie's new London Bridge, in 1831, and the demolition of the old medieval one, drew another line between past and present. Wider bridge arches increased the flow of the river, consigning the picturesque Frost Fairs to the history books. As well as new bridges over the Thames, Marc Isambard Brunel's workmen were busy beneath the riverbed, building the Thames Tunnel between Wapping and Rotherhithe. Constructed between 1825 and 1843, it was the world's first tunnel under a navigable waterway.

Processions of ceremonial barges remained a feature of the river. However, the Thames was becoming polluted with chemical waste and human excrement. Cholera and typhoid fever were prevalent in the insanitary, low-lying, riverside districts. Political change impacted on the port area. The dock companies armed themselves heavily against expected attacks from radicals. Despite the strong opposition of London's powerful West India lobby, slavery was abolished in the British colonies after more than 200 years.

The last Frost Fair on the Thames, held in the winter of 1814

The City Barge

Searle & Godfrey, of Stangate, Lambeth, supplied this large-scale builders' model of the last City barge of 1807 to the City Corporation. Some 24.4 metres (eighty foot) long, and with a beam of just over 4.3 metres (fourteen foot), the City barge was one of the largest ceremonial craft ever built. The cabin was richly decorated on the outside with both the Royal and City coats of arms. The interior was sumptuously finished in red and gold paintwork and upholstery. Like most later barges, it had a strong roof to the cabin for the better accommodation of passengers and musicians. The model shows the raised and tapered lute stern, ornamented with carvings of Neptune and Amphitrite supporting the City arms. This splendid barge cost the Corporation £2579.

Crewed by eighteen watermen, a mate and the barge master, the City barge conveyed incoming Lord Mayors to Westminster, as part of the annual procession, and attended other riverborne public occasions. Ceremonial barges were built with the hull shape of watermen's wherries. They are first mentioned in 1422, when one was hired by the incoming Lord Mayor. The City barge was last used for the Lord Mayor's Procession in 1856. In that year the Corporation lost its conservancy responsibilities for the now very polluted river to the Thames Conservancy. The Corporation disposed of the barge in 1859 for £85.

Searle and Godfrey specialised in building, storing and repairing ceremonial barges, as well as racing boats, wherries and skiffs. In 1817 they built an early Thames paddle steamer, the *London*. They occupied extensive premises at Stangate until the mid-1860s, when their yard was demolished to make way for St Thomas's Hospital.

Builders' model of the last City Barge, 1807

Elizabeth Walton

This portrait in oils of Elizabeth Walton (1762–1832) was painted around 1830. Elizabeth was married to John Charles Kitching (1760 –1844), the last Tide Carpenter of Old London Bridge. Responsible for the piled starlings, Kitching enjoyed 'great profit.' He and his wife twice had their portraits painted. Elizabeth is shown wearing a fashionable blue-green dress and a coral necklace. The artist has made Elizabeth's face appear younger than a woman in her mid-sixties. The baby boy also wears a dress and a coral necklace. The latter were popular for children, being thought to ward off evil.

Elizabeth Walton, portrait around 1830

Whaling journal

Whaling journal, from the *Mary*, 1823–1825

This is a journal from the London South Sea whaler, the *Mary*, on a voyage in the years 1823 to 1825. The ship was owned by the London merchant John Lydekker and commanded by Edward Reed Lacy. The journal records details of the ship's course, the weather and other events. Black tails, or flukes, indicate whale kills. A grinning whale's head records misses. The journal also includes details of individual harpooners and the barrels of oil recovered from each catch. The *Mary* had an eventful voyage whaling in the South Atlantic and the Pacific. Three crewmen were lost when a whaleboat was destroyed in a storm. The crew suffered from scurvy and a number absconded. The ship was wrecked on Jervis's Island on 20 January 1825. After six weeks, two London whaling ships – the *Francis* and the *Vansittart* – belonging to Daniel Bennett, rescued the crew.

Works at St Katharine Docks

W Ranwell's watercolour of the building of St Katharine Docks, 1828

The last of the twenty-one year monopolies granted to the three major dock companies expired in 1827. In anticipation of this a group of merchants, shipowners and financiers, led by John Hall, established the St Katharine Dock Company. The Company decided to build its new dock as close as possible to the 'seat of commerce' in the City. It chose an already built-up 9.5 hectares (23.5 acre) site immediately east of the Tower. Despite intensive opposition from the London Dock Company, wharfingers and inhabitants, the Company was granted an enabling Act of Parliament in 1825.

Around 1250 houses were torn down and 11,000 inhabitants displaced without compensation. The medieval buildings of the Royal Hospital and Collegiate Church of St Katharine-by-the-Tower were demolished. Even so, the site was small and awkward. Thomas Telford, the engineer, and Philip Hardwicke, the architect, provided an ingenious solution. Two docks, with warehouses rising sheer from their sides on cast-iron columns, were to be linked to an entrance lock via a ship basin.

Excavation work began in May 1826. W Ranwell's watercolour, completed in January 1828,

vividly captures the reality of early dock building. At the time over 1000 labourers, masons, bricklayers, carters and engineers were busy at work. The docks were excavated entirely by hand. Spoil was removed by wheelbarrows and in horse-drawn wagons on iron railways. That not needed to raise the quayside was barged to Pimlico for land reclamation. Ranwell took his view from the south-eastern end of the entrance basin, looking towards the City. The entrance lock and the cuttings to the western and eastern docks are all visible. The docks were formally opened on 25 October 1828.

Dock Company arms

The London dock companies appointed their own constables and watchmen from the beginning. They were usually armed only with wooden truncheons and staves. During times of civil unrest, however, constables, watchmen and special constables were also armed with guns, boarding pikes and swords. The dock companies took extra defensive measures during the events surrounding the Reform Act (1830–1832) and the final phase of the Chartist movement (1848). In January 1832, the West India Dock Company established an Armed Watch of 100 dock workers, supported by a 100-strong band of special

Dock company weapons, 1830–1850

constables, to defend its property against radical political activists. The watch had muskets and its officers had swords and 'a brace of pistols.' The specials had cutlasses and truncheons.

In 1848 the St Katharine Dock Company had a store of 249 pikes, 175 cutlasses, seventy-five pistols and twenty-four muskets. The expected attacks on London's docks never materialised.

Jamaican treadmill

Engraving of a Jamaican treadmill, 1836

a widespread campaign of opposition. This engraving promoted a tract by James Williams, 'an Apprenticed Labourer in Jamaica.' It shows exhausted men and women on a treadmill, having their legs whipped. One woman has collapsed. Women field workers, chained together and carrying hoes, pass under the watchful eyes of two plantation owners. Intended to run for six years, the apprenticeship system was abolished after four. In 1834 there were 311,692 slaves in Jamaica and 469,301 in the remainder of the colonies.

When slavery was abolished in the British colonies, in 1834, it was replaced by an invidious system of 'apprenticeship' for ex-slaves. This bound them to their ex-owners to work on a subsistence basis. Abolitionists mounted

Sailortown
1840–1850

St Katharine's, Wapping, Shadwell, Ratcliffe, Limehouse, Poplar, Bermondsey, Rotherhithe, Deptford, Greenwich, Woolwich and Gravesend all catered for sailors. This was the land of 'Jack Ashore'. The most famous 'Sailortown' quarter encompassed Wapping, Shadwell and Ratcliff Highway. A maze of streets, lanes and alleys backed the riverside wharves and docks. There, were to be found ship chandlers, curio sellers, slop sellers, sailors' lodging houses, alehouses, ginshops, brothels, slum houses, cook shops, wild animal shops and pawnshops.

Sailortown's rich mix of foreign seamen and residents fascinated many commentators. They compared the appearance and language of sailors from around the world with those of the British 'Jack Tar'. Writers also drew attention to the exploitative nature of Sailortown and its 'land sharks'. Their strongest criticisms were directed at crimps, prostitutes and bullies. Crimps met incoming sailors, taking them to their own lodging houses and pubs, providing them with prostitutes and encouraging them to run up debts. Prostitutes and their bullies, or protectors, were seen as only intent on 'cleaning out' defenceless sailors.

Reality was somewhat different. Sailors were not exactly innocents abroad. There were many respectable lodging houses and pubs. Most women were not prostitutes. Those that were, often had no bullies and enjoyed live-in relationships with individual sailors – their 'husbands' while in port.

The rise of philanthropic sailors' homes, missions, temperance halls, steamships and new docks saw the gradual decline of the old Sailortown districts.

A scene in a Sailortown pub, around 1830

Sailortown street

The Sailortown Gallery recreates many aspects of Wapping in the 1840s and 1850s. Those brave enough to visit found the area around Ratcliffe Highway 'at once both foul and picturesque'. The Reverend Thomas Beames, writing in 1852, offered the best contemporary description:

'Go there by day and every fourth man you meet is a sailor... Public houses abound in these localities... they are interspersed with shops also peculiar to such districts...

from the capitalists, whose ample window is hung round with everything which can catch a sailor's eye, or sound the depths of his pocket, to the small retail tradesman... who depends almost for bread upon his daily earnings. Ship joiners – ship carpenters – mathematical instrument makers, with their sign-posts of gilded captains peering through telescopes, – provision shops, – rope makers – vendors of ship biscuits, even ship booksellers, – ironmongers –

dealers in marine stores, are strangely mixed together.

'Public houses occur at frequent intervals... these centres of attraction are fitted up with everything which can draw sailors together... In a third class of houses were professional thieves... they were evidently preying upon the drunken sailors whose ill luck had led them to places with whose abominations they were little acquainted. Women of the town were in league with these men...'

Reconstruction of a Sailortown street, around 1840 to 50

Sailors' lodging house

Reconstruction of a sailors' lodging house, around 1840–1850

Most seamen stayed in common lodging houses. The Reverend Thomas Beames made a point of examining some of these:

'... In all districts where sailors abound, there are several of these harpies (crimps) and their lodging-houses – and that of these places there are successive graduations, from decent looking houses to the lowest dens of infamy... One of these houses was inspected, which seemed a decent specimen of the class; the landlord was a foreigner, and it was a rendezvous for French, Italians, Germans, Spaniards, Portuguese and Greeks. On the ground floor, there was a small common room, garnished with prints on nautical subjects; a very fine macaw was flapping his wings at one end... On the first floor were three rooms... fitted up, like the cabins of steamers, with tiers... the payment for the accommodation thus afforded, was 12s a week... bed and board but not spirits.

'We crossed the road and came upon another back street in which were several lodging houses. In the first of these, in the rooms we entered, were seven or eight people sleeping... Sheets seemed scarce things, in many of the houses there were no beds, but only mattresses strewed on the floor, and a few blankets thrown over the sleepers... 1½ d per night is the usual charge... In all places where sailors resort they seem to create such dens... they are prey of a vast number of designing persons, male and female, of the lowest description, who gather round them the moment they are discharged, and who live by preying on them.'

35

First Port of Empire
1840–1939

London benefited enormously from its position as the trading heart of the British Empire. Between 1855 and 1886, a series of important new docks were opened to accommodate steamships. The progressive removal of selected Customs duties, from the 1840s, encouraged the rebuilding of river wharves. The 'free water clause' enabled lighters to enter the docks free of charge. By the 1870s, the wharves were siphoning off around three-quarters of dock imports.

The riverside east and west of the City attracted large-scale industry, including shipyards, engineering works, potteries, gasworks and soap and candleworks. Iron shipbuilding and engine-making expanded rapidly in the 1840s and 1850s, at the Isle of Dogs, Bow Creek and Greenwich. Isambard Kingdom Brunel's *Great Eastern* was launched at John Scott Russell's Millwall Yard in 1858.

The riverside still supported communities of fishermen, some of whom fished the river, while others fished for cod in distant waters. Heavy pollution of the river ruined the livelihood of the former, endangered the lives of Londoners and resulted in the building of Joseph Bazalgette's massive interceptor sewers in the 1860s. The working and living conditions of many riverside communities deteriorated due to economic changes. Competition between the dock companies and the riverside wharves was intense, to the detriment of the casual workforce. The frustrations of many workers erupted during the 1889 Dock Strike. The creation of the Port of London Authority (PLA) in 1909 brought a much-needed rationalisation to port activities.

Photograph of South West India Dock, opened in 1870

Shipwright's tools

Shipwright's chest, with tools, 1850–1900

This painted tool chest, adze, axe and caulking tools belonged to the Somerville family. The chest contains shipwrights' and ship joiners' tools. From their makers' stamps, most of the woodworking planes can be dated from 1850 to 1900. The chest and the other tools are also from this period. The Somerville family worked across the three main traditional wooden shipbuilding trades of shipwright, ship joiner and caulker. Shipwrights built the main 'carcass' of the ship from 'keel to gunwale.' Ship joiners fitted up the interior, including cabins and stairways. Caulkers drove oakum, or spun yarn, into the seams of the hull and deck planking. The seams were then covered with hot pitch to make them watertight. Traditionally, the phrases 'river built' and 'Blackwall fashion' were a guarantee of the highest quality vessels.

In 1850, Henry Mayhew, the social observer, estimated that London had around 2000 wooden shipwrights, 350 ship joiners, 250 mast- and block-makers, 150 barge-builders and 100 boat-builders. Mayhew found London shipwrights to be intelligent, well-off family men who built the best ships in the world. The tradesmen all purchased their own tools. Mayhew reckoned that a complete set of shipwright's tools cost two pounds and ten shillings, and one for ship joiners cost twenty pounds. Many shipwrights belonged to the Shipwrights Provident Union of the Port of London. Wooden shipwrights sarcastically referred to the growing band of iron shipbuilders as 'boilermakers.' Iron shipbuilding had developed rapidly in the 1840s and was soon to transform the London industry, from one based on artisan skills to one based on heavy engineering. The distinctive ring of caulking hammers was overshadowed by the sound of steamhammers. The skills of traditional shipwrights, caulkers, ship joiners, block-makers and figurehead carvers were still required to fit out iron ships.

The *Princess Alice* nameplate

PRINCESS ALICE

Princess Alice nameplate, salvaged in 1878

Downriver trips on Thames paddle steamers had been popular with Londoners since 1815. By 1876, the new London Steamboat Company had a fleet of seventy steamers. Two years later, their *Princess Alice* sunk in what remains the worst marine disaster in British coastal waters. On 3 September, at 7.40 on a clear evening, the *Princess Alice* was a kilometre and a half (one mile) below Woolwich, on her way back from Sheerness. On board were more than 800 people, many of whom had enjoyed a day out at Rosherville Gardens, Gravesend. At the same time, the much larger steam collier, the *Bywell Castle* was making her way downriver. The two vessels were set to pass safely when the *Princess Alice* suddenly turned to port, bringing herself across the bows of the *Bywell Castle*. In the ensuing collision, the paddle steamer was nearly cut in two and sank within five minutes, drowning 640 passengers.

This brass nameplate was discovered in the Port of London Authority Collection. It was possibly removed by the Thames Conservancy, which raised the vessel in conjunction with Trinity House. When the sections of the *Princess Alice* were beached at Woolwich, they attracted thousands of spectators and souvenir hunters.

Lambeth stoneware

Many industries were attracted to London's riverside, east and west of the City. The riverside offered space for larger industrial operations and facilitated the import of raw materials and the export of finished products. Stoneware potteries were located at Fulham, Mortlake, Vauxhall and Lambeth.

The greatest concentration of stoneware makers was at Lambeth. By 1860 Lambeth's stoneware potteries had seventy kilns. Barges and lighters delivered coal and clay and carrried products for export. As well as producing

Lambeth stoneware products, 1840–1845

utilitarian items like jars, bottles and pots, Lambeth potteries also made decorative wares. W Northern probably made the fish spirit flask in about 1840; Doulton & Watts made the Nelson jug around 1845; about the same time, Stephen Green's Imperial Potteries made the tipstaff flask.

39

Barking fish carrier

The period 1820 to 1870 saw the Barking fishing fleet at its zenith. In 1850 Barking had 220 smacks, employing 1370 men and boys. Smacks fished the Thames Estuary, the Dogger Bank, the North Sea and Icelandic waters, long-lining and trawling for cod. Each smack carried a crew of nine to eleven men and boys. Originally, the smacks had wet wells to bring live catches to Billingsgate Market. The Hewett family introduced many improvements to cod fishing, including the fleeting system, the use of ice and fast fish carriers. In the 1860s, some eighteen fast fish carriers serviced the North Sea fleet,

Model of the Barking fish carrier, *Ranger*, built in 1864

carrying boxes of fish packed in ice to London. Excellent sailors to windward, these sleek cutters were built for

hard work. The model depicts the 22.9 metres (75 foot) long *Ranger*, built in 1864, most probably at Barking.

Henry Thomas Lambert

George Townsend Cole (1810–1883) painted this oil portrait of Henry Thomas Lambert in 1858. The 1859 *London Post Office Directory* listed Lambert as 'Sailmaker & Ship Chandler at 307 High Street, Wapping', close to London Docks. Cole's splendid portrait is a rare depiction of a well-off London tradesman, and part of his home, when it was still not uncommon to 'live above the shop'.

The soberly dressed Lambert is depicted reading a copy of the *Times*, seated in a

mahogany elbow chair of around 1840. This matches the side chairs in the bay window and is of similar date to the overmantel and fender. Most of the furnishings, however, are contemporary with the painting. These include the stylish serpentine mahogany side cabinet, the vases, the wax fruit, the glass lustre and the 'gasolier' or ceiling gas lamp.

Through the window can be glimpsed the Bermondsey waterfront and the busy river. This view also shows

shipping and craft, which provided Lambert with his comfortable lifestyle. Cole's painting intentionally acknowledges this.

The well-known American artist, James McNeill Whistler, captured the workaday aspect of London's river at this period in his *Thames Series* of etchings. Few viewers of Whistler's etchings would have realised that interiors like Lambert's lay within the apparently ramshackle riverside facades.

Henry Thomas Lambert by George Townsend Cole, 1858. Purchased in 1995, with the assistance of the National Art Collections Fund and the Victoria & Albert Museum

Tilbury Docks' invitation

By 1850, new docks for steamships were badly needed. These were eventually provided through a programme of massive, but competitive, capital investment. Between 1855 and 1900, London's dock system doubled in size. The independent Victoria Dock opened in 1855, on the Canning Town marshes. A separate dock company opened the Millwall Dock in 1868. The London and St Katharine Dock Company opened the Royal Albert Dock in 1880. The East and West India Dock Company countered by creating Tilbury Docks, forty-two kilometres (twenty-six miles) downstream of London Bridge, built between 1882 and 1886.

This chromo-lithographic invitation was issued for the docks' formal opening in April 1886. Tilbury Docks were designed for the rapid transit of cargoes. Goods and passengers were transferred to London by railway.

Invitation to the opening of the Tilbury Docks, 1886

'Billies and Charlies'

London's Victorian antiquarians closely watched all new building and engineering works for archaeological discoveries. When the Shadwell Dock was being built at the London Docks in 1857, two enterprising labourers manufactured their own finds. William Smith and Charles Eaton helped dig the dock's foundations. Soon their fake 'medieval' lead badges and figures were being eagerly purchased. The question of their authenticity split the antiquarian fraternity, with the leading archaeologist, Charles Roach Smith, declaring them 'genuine relics.' Smith and

Fake antiquities, known as 'Billies and Charlies', around 1857–1860

Eaton supplied one dealer with over 1600 figures for £346. Their 'finds' were finally exposed as fakes in 1860, when one of the casting moulds was discovered. The forgeries, also 'discovered' from Blackfriars to Hampton Court, continued to be made until the 1870s.

Stevedores' banner

Rotherhithe stevedores' banner, around 1905

Large painted banners had been used in processions of trade guilds and friendly societies in the early nineteenth century. They were adopted by the first trade unions representing skilled workers. By the end of the century they were popular with the new unions, representing less skilled workers. During the 1889 Dock Strike, some forty banners were carried on the huge daily marches from the East India Docks to the City. Although the five-week strike began at the South West India Dock, it quickly spread to all other port workers, and to London coalmen, carters and engineers' labourers. The main aim of the strike, however, was to raise the dock labourers' hourly pay from five pence to six, to create a minimum daily wage of two shillings, and to regularise piecework rates.

In the year after the successful Dock Strike, banners were made in great numbers for new branches of the different port unions. Most were supplied by George Tutill of City Road, the largest bannermaker. Union branches often had ceremonial public 'unfurling' ceremonies for their new banners. This striking banner was made around 1905, by Tutill, for Branch Number Six (Rotherhithe) of the Amalgamated Stevedores' Labour Protection League. The painted panel commemorates the crucial financial support that Australia provided for the near-starving dockers. A London stevedore shakes hands with an Australian 'wharfie' in front of Britannia and the British lion. A steamer, a fully rigged ship, a lighter and a sailing barge fill the river behind. The panel symbolises the international brotherhood of labour, the British Empire and the might of London shipping.

Warehouse of the World
1840–1939

The open quaysides, transit sheds and towering warehouses that lined the docks and riverside housed every conceivable commodity. Here were spices and drugs; grain, sugar, meat and fruit; coffee, cocoa and tea; wines, spirits and tobacco; shells, furs and feathers; leather, skins and hide; timber, paper and jute; wool and oriental carpets, and more. Imports were dominated by Empire produce.

These cargoes were carried to London by a wide variety of ships. As the nineteenth century progressed, growing competition from steamships encouraged improvements to the square-rigged sailing ship. In the years 1840 to 1875, sleek and fast 'clippers' were built. Clippers carried tea from China and later, wool from Australia. From 1875, much heavier four-masted 'barques' were built as bulk carriers for wool, grain and nitrate. By the late 1880s, however, steam had overtaken sail.

For many cargoes, London dominated the UK trade. In the 1930s, London handled around 90 per cent of all imported tea and 80 per cent of imported wool. Tobacco, timber, grain, sugar, wines and spirits were other important cargoes. The Port of London Authority (PLA) and riverside wharfingers employed skilled samplers, who prepared lots for sale at City auction houses. The old East India Company's Cutler Street Warehouses, close to Houndsditch, were the PLA's main town warehouses. These, together with the London and St Katharine Docks, handled some of the port's most exotic and interesting cargoes. Most warehouses in the port had their own special feel and smell.

Inspecting bales of cinnamon at No. 6 Warehouse, London Docks, in 1898

The *Torrens*

Sailor-made model of the *Torrens*, around 1890

The square-rigged ship, the *Torrens*, was built in Sunderland in 1875. Owned in London, she operated on the Australian run and was broken up in 1910. This late nineteenth century 'sailor made' model was probably built by one of the ship's own crew. As with other models of this type, the rigging details are accurate, but the masts and spars are over scale. The general finish of the hull and deck details are fairly crude. Still, the model has enormous charm.

The *Torrens* is especially famous because the celebrated writer Joseph Conrad joined her as First Mate in 1891. At the time, Conrad was living in London and struggling to write his first novel, *Almayer's Folly*. Conrad retained a fondness for the ship, writing in 1926 that:

'The Torrens had a fame which attracted the right kind of sailor, and when engaging her crew her chief officer had always a large and promising crowd to pick and choose from... for apart from her more brilliant qualities, such as her speed and her celebrated good looks (which by themselves go a long way with a sailor), she was regarded as a 'comfortable ship' in a strictly professional sense, which means that she was known to handle easily and to be a good sea boat in heavy weather.'

Conrad left the *Torrens*, in October 1893, and retired from the sea. Big square-riggers, like the *Torrens*, carried bales of wool from Australian ports to the London Docks at Wapping.

Opium pipe

This mid-nineteenth century opium pipe was confiscated from a Chinese seaman in one of the enclosed docks. The wooden box which contained it formed a secret compartment in the sailor's bunk. Extracted from the Asian poppy, opium is a strong narcotic drug inducing a trance-like stupor. Opium was smoked by some of the Chinese community in Limehouse and visiting sailors. Writers and journalists greatly exaggerated the existence of 'opium dens' in the area.

Mid-nineteenth century Chinese opium pipe

Opium was grown extensively as a cash crop in British India and exported by fast opium clippers to China. Chinese concern about their trading balance – rather than drug addiction – led to the 'Opium Wars' of 1839 to 1842, and 1856 to 1860. The Chinese lost Hong Kong to the British and were forced to open more ports to foreign trade. Although the British forcibly exported opium to China, its use at home was regarded as 'sinful.'

The Strangers' Home

Photograph of the Strangers' Home, Limehouse, around 1900

Sailors from all corners of the globe visited London, the world's largest port until 1935. Most seamen found lodgings in and around Docklands. From the mid-nineteenth century, the opening of large sailors' homes helped improve living conditions.

Most Asian seamen coming to London stayed in lodging-houses and homes in Limehouse and Poplar. In some lodging-houses, conditions were very poor, with seamen sharing beds in backyard sheds. The most 'reputable' Asian sailors stayed at the 'Strangers' Home for Asiatics, Africans, and South Sea Islanders,' Limehouse. Opened in 1857, this had bedrooms, kitchens, reading rooms and dining rooms. In 1900, the writer Count Armfelt reported that:

'...There you may see Indians, Burmese, Arabs, Japanese, Chinese, Malays, Singalese, Zanzibars, Sumatrans and other Orientals, for the 'Strangers' Home'... admits all creeds, all races, all castes and all callings.'

Import samples

Thousands of different commodities came into the Port of London and its seemingly endless warehouses. The dock companies provided sampling facilities and special sample rooms, for merchants and brokers, at their main offices and town warehouses. 'Sample berths' were sited around the docks themselves. Samplers were all highly skilled. The imports seen here are displayed in a black painted sample cabinet stamped with the initials of the East and West India Dock Company (1838–1901). The case would have displayed a reference collection, possibly at the Company's 'Museum' at the

Victorian import samples

West India Docks.

The docks offered an object lesson in commercial geography. When the journalist Millicent Morrison visited the London Docks in 1897, she was taken aback by:

'...The endless offspring of the animal, vegetable and mineral kingdom brought hither from both sea and land to render willing service to civilised man. They tell of a world-wide industry centred here in epitome – the Emporium of the World.'

Dockers

Dockers trucking oranges, 1931

This photograph, taken in July 1931, shows dockers trucking boxes of the first season's South African oranges in a West India Dock transit shed. The cargo had just been unloaded from the *Dunbar Castle*. The dockers included both permanent and casual men. In 1931, there were 37,000 registered dockworkers in London, down from 61,000 in 1921. In 1931, daily unemployment in the port was around thirty-percent. Casual dockers earned a basic twelve shillings a day and the 3000 PLA permanent men earned sixty-six shillings a week. Pay had dropped by a quarter since 1921.

Dock hooks

Different types of dock hooks had evolved to handle particular cargoes. Efficient hooks were essential for stevedores and dockers, who had to move cargoes speedily, especially when doing piecework. There were a number of hooks in common use. Stevedores' single 'S' hooks were used on crates, timber and sets of cargoes. The pronounced bend, above the handle, was designed to protect the knuckles. Less pronounced single dock, or 'Colonial', hooks were used for bag work. Large double pronged hooks were used for bales. Hooks similar to these were in use in Roman London.

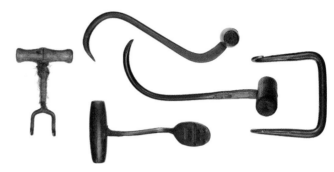

Stevedores and dockers hooks, around 1930

'Catspaw' or pad hooks were used in pairs to handle bags of fine material such as flour. Pairs of wooden handled double bag hooks were used on less fine commodities, such as coffee beans. Stevedores and dockers all owned their own single hooks, usually buying them, or having them made, when they started work. Personal hooks were jealously guarded and often handed down in the family. The hooks seen here date back to around 1930.

Paddle steamer

Model of the Thames paddle steamer, *Royal Eagle*, built in 1932

Many port activities were hidden away from ordinary Londoners behind tall dock walls. River steamers provided a good opportunity to see shipping, riverside warehouses and dock entrances. The period between 1919 and 1939 was the heyday of the big Thames passenger steamers. Thousands of sightseers and holidaymakers were carried between London and the coastal resorts of Southend, Clacton, Herne Bay, Margate and Ramsgate. This model depicts the *Royal Eagle*, the pride of the General Steam Navigation Company's fleet. Cammell Laird & Company, Birkenhead, built the steamer in 1932. Described as a 'miniature liner', she could carry up to 1987 passengers.

Thames Gallery
1850–1950

Boats, barges, tugs and ships were the lifeblood of London. This gallery presents working and pleasure boats, ship models, and reconstructions of premises that supported port activities.

The Thames continued to be home to a variety of working boats. In the rougher and busier waters below Chelsea Bridge, the most common boat was the waterman's skiff. Above Chelsea Bridge, watermen used much lighter 'hiring' skiffs. In 1910, there were some 500 licensed passenger-carrying skiffs on the river. A wide range of pleasure boats was in use on the river above Richmond. Small double-ended peterboats were still fishing at Putney and Strand-on-the-Green. Downriver, larger bawley boats fished for shrimps from Gravesend and Leigh-on-Sea.

In the 1930s Londoners had many opportunities to see the 1000 ships which visited the port each week. Below London Bridge, splendid liners jostled for space with tramp cargo carriers, short-sea traders, coasters, steam colliers, grain racers, Mediterranean traders, cable ships and moored school training ships. In addition to the ships, the river was home to large fleets of tugs, barges and sailing barges. Conversant with all aspects of craft handling and river currents, tugmen and lightermen knew the location of hundreds of riverside wharves. Along the river were the many depots, workshops and other premises serving the needs of the port. Foremost amongst these were those belonging to the PLA and the Corporation of Trinity House, jointly responsible for the maintenance of good and safe navigation in the port.

Poster depicting a Wapping waterman, around 1920

Buoy bell cage

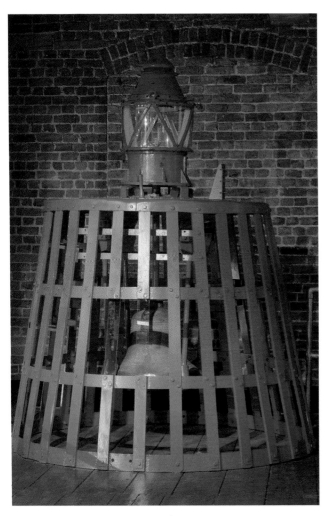

Reconstruction of a buoy bell cage, around 1900–1930

The maintenance of good and safe navigation for shipping is an essential requirement of a major port. Trinity House retained its historic responsibility for the main Thames Estuary navigation buoys and lights – as well as ship pilotage – after the establishment of the Port of London Authority (PLA), in 1909. The PLA was responsible for maintaining buoys and lights within the port area.

This composite reconstruction of an early twentieth century 'lighted bell buoy superstructure' has been assembled from components collected from Trinity Buoy Wharf, Blackwall. The 'can' style cage would have been bolted to a large 5.1 tonnes (five ton) floating hemispherical buoy, anchored by a sinker weight. The bronze bell was made at J Warner's London bell foundry in 1902. Four external 'bellhammers', suspended on thick rubber pads, struck warnings for shipping during foggy weather. They were activated as the buoy swayed on the constantly moving river. Carbide cylinders stored inside the buoy powered thc signal lamp. Carbide gas – used extensively from the beginning of the century – emitted a white light.

Trinity Buoy Wharf offered one of the most fascinating sights on the river. The quay was always crowded with marker buoys in a rich variety of sizes, shapes and colours. Bell cages, buoy chains and concrete sinkers were also stored and repaired there. Trinity House tenders and light vessels came there for repair. The Wharf had extensive workshops for blacksmiths, engineers and tinsmiths and covered stores. An experimental lighthouse, built in 1864 to 1866, was used to test new light mechanisms and to train lighthouse keepers. A Trinity House depot was on the site by 1810. It eventually came to serve the area between Southwold, in Suffolk, and Dungeness in Kent. Trinity Buoy Wharf closed in 1988, destined never again to 'make bad buoys good.'

Diving

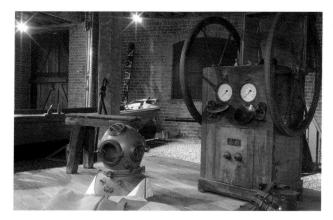

Reconstruction of a diving platform, around 1950

operated in the dark and muddy waters of the Thames and docks, salvaging sunken craft, repairing damage to dredgers and clearing fouled propellers. They also worked on underwater dock plant and piles. Each year, divers checked the chains on 340 mooring buoys. Every dive was inherently dangerous. Divers worked from wreck-raising lighters, large skiffs and floating platforms. This small reconstruction of a diving platform, around 1930 to 1950, is dressed with a canvas diving suit, helmet, weights and boots. The manual air pump, made by Siebe, Gorman & Co, pumped fresh air to the diver.

The PLA's responsibilities for navigation included dredging the river channels, raising wrecks and laying down mooring buoys. Much of this work involved the PLA's teams of divers and their assistants. These highly skilled men

Pleasure skiff

Between 1870 and 1914, the Thames above Richmond was a great pleasure resort. Regattas, fêtes, rowing, punting and sailing were all immensely popular. Boat-builders and watermen hired out skiffs, gigs, punts and canoes. This six-person, double-sculling, mahogany pleasure skiff dates to the 1880s and was probably built by E. Messum & Sons, Richmond. In 1895 she was called *Ethel* and licensed to Charles Shore, of Water Lane, Twickenham. From 1898 and 1939 she was called *Lady of the Lake*, before becoming the *Jilanjon*. Between 1951

The pleasure skiff, *Jilanjon*, built around 1885

and 1956 she was owned by the Twickenham waterman, Thomas Haynes, who sold her to Walter Hammerton & Co. The *Jilanjon* was also registered as a ferry skiff.

Rigger's workshop

Riggers made and repaired both ships' rigging and cargo handling gear. Their practical knowledge of ropework, including hundreds of knots and splices, helped ensure the safety of ships, people and cargoes. Until the introduction of wire rope, in the mid-nineteenth century, natural fibre ropes were universally used on board ships, on the quaysides and in warehouses.

This reconstructed workshop, or 'loft', contains many of the tools and products of the rigger. An axe and block were used for cutting natural rope to length. The process of splicing rope together began by 'whipping' the ends of the strands with twine, to stop them fraying. The rope was then opened up, with a conical wooden 'fid', so that a strand could be woven through to begin the splice. Big 'set' fids, standing on the floor, were used for large ropes, such as mooring cables. Fids were usually made of very hard *lignum vitae*. Wire rope was spliced with the aid of a steel 'marline spike' and a rigger's vice. Splices were often protected by a layer of canvas and cord, wound on with a 'serving board.' Riggers also made cargo nets, the linings of cargo baskets, fenders, bosun's chairs and Jacob's ladders. Many tools were common to both riggers and sailmakers, especially the benches and wooden fids.

Historically, rigging lofts – like the closely associated sail

Reconstruction of a rigger's workshop, around 1930

lofts – usually occupied the attics of buildings where there were large open working floors. There were many independent rigging lofts, but they were also found at shipyards. In the enclosed docks they were usually attached to the gear stores, on the ground floor of a building. Traditionally, many

riggers learned the essentials of their trade as seamen. Work in rigging lofts then widened their skills. In large establishments, loft riggers made up the different elements of ship and cargo rigging. Outdoor riggers fitted their work up and carried out repairs.

The *Mark Lane* steam tug

Model of the craft tug *Mark Lane*, built in 1923
(Courtesy of the National Maritime Museum London)

In addition to the 1000 ships which visited the Port of London each week in the 1930s, the river was home to a fleet of 350 tugs, 500 sailing barges and 8000 lighters and barges. These worked at everything from transporting valuable cargoes between the lower docks and riverside wharves, to carrying away the city's refuse to landfill sites.

This model is of the craft towing steam tug, the *Mark Lane*, built at Selby in 1923 for the Tilbury Contracting & Dredging Company. The tug was 22.7 metres (74.6 foot) in length and 82.3 tonnes (81 tons) gross weight. She was named after the location of the company's City office. By the mid-1930s the company had a fleet of modern craft towing tugs and 140 lighters, carrying around 700,000 tons of cargo a year.

Challis's Bakery

Up and down the river, a wide range of small businesses catered to the many needs of the port and its communities.

This reconstructed bakehouse is from Challis's bakery and confectionery shop, Station Road, Greenhithe, in Kent. The Challises operated the bakery between 1915 and 1989. Greenhithe was a busy riverside village and the base for Everard's fleet of coasters and barges. Challis's made bread, pies and cakes for villagers, riverside workers and those in the local cement works. It also provided for the nearby training ships.

Bakehouse reconstruction, around 1930

55

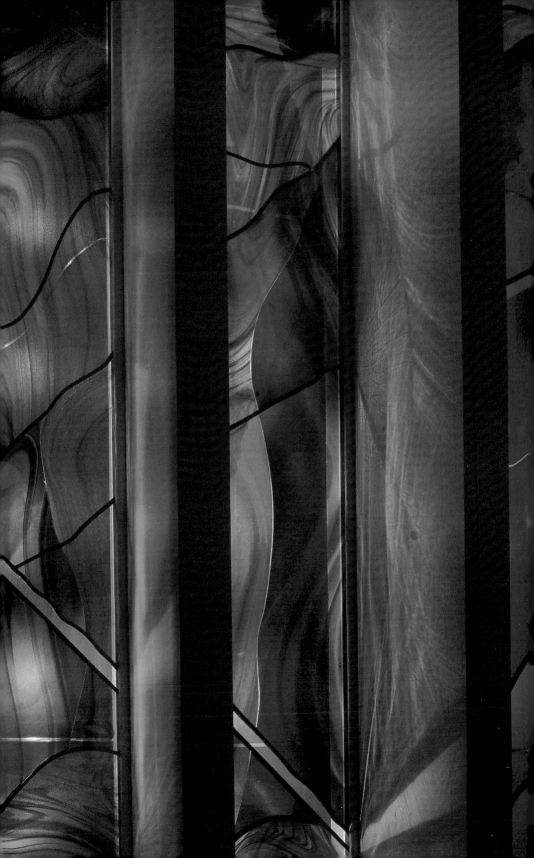

Dockland at War
1939–1945

The port and its communities bore the brunt of enemy attack during the Second World War. They also played a vital part in Britain's fight-back. When war was declared, few Londoners were surprised. A Port Emergency Committee had existed since 1936, and the Port of London Authority (PLA) had built 200 shelters.

London tugs, sailing barges and launches assisted in the evacuation of troops from Dunkirk in May 1940. On the afternoon of 7 September 1940 – 'Black Saturday' – the *Luftwaffe* targeted riverside works and the docks. Fire and smoke from incendiary and high explosive bombs soon silhouetted the river. The Blitz had begun and continuous night bombing was to last for thirteen weeks. The docks, factories and residential communities suffered extensive damage, destruction and fatalities. Civil defence and fire fighting units were kept constantly occupied. Anti-aircraft guns and barrage balloons protected the river approaches.

Dockyards and riverside factories, many now employing more women in the workforce, supported the war effort. Tate & Lyle manufactured aeroplane parts as well as refined sugar. Cable works produced much of the Pipe Line Under the Ocean (PLUTO), used to supply fuel oil for the Allied advance from Normandy in 1944. Many of the Phoenix Units of the Mulberry Harbours, used at the Normandy landings in June 1944, were built in the docks and along the river. Over 23,000 vessels and craft were converted, maintained and repaired. Even after victory was in sight, attacks by V1 and V2 rockets brought further destruction to the area in 1944 and 1945.

War and Peace, stained glass installation, John Patsalides Studios, 2002

William Ware and *The Human Chain*

The Human Chain, painting by William Ware, 1940 (Courtesy Martin Ware)

William Ware (1915–1997) began painting at the age of nine, while in a hospital for 'incurables.' He had suffered a broken back when he was three and his condition appears to have been further complicated by contracting tuberculosis. As a result, he received no early formal education. When he was sixteen, a pioneering operation cured his spinal injury. A year later he enrolled at Putney Art School and then won a scholarship to Richmond School of Art. In 1938 he embarked on a career as a commercial artist.

At the outbreak of the war, Ware was prevented from joining the armed forces by his earlier injuries. Instead, he worked at his brother-in-law's plastics factory. By night, he painted and sketched the Blitz from the rooftops. The river and docks held a special fascination and he refused to take shelter during air-raid attacks. Ware's first wartime painting was purchased by the Imperial War Museum in 1939. In 1941 he sold his painting *Fired City* to the Ministry of Information, on the recommendation of the War Artists' Advisory Committee. During the Blitz he became friendly with the artist David Bomberg.

Ware's painting, *The Human Chain*, was completed in 1940. It depicts rescue and salvage crews at work in a bombed warehouse or industrial building. Like his ten other paintings on view in the Museum, it chillingly captures the devastation caused by enemy bombing. After the war, Ware pursued a successful career as an artist and gallery owner.

Molten column

Late in the afternoon of Saturday 7 September 1940, the *Luftwaffe* launched a massive daylight raid on London. Ninety continuous night-time raids followed. London's docks and riverside wharves were prime targets for enemy bombers. Incendiary bombs, designed to start fires quickly, were particularly effective. Most dock warehouses had timber interiors and these quickly ignited. Many cargoes were extremely flammable. As windows blew out, air and wind fuelled the fires, creating infernos.

This section of a molten cast-iron Victorian warehouse column, from the London Docks, bears remarkable witness to the intense heat of fires started by incendiary bombs. The temperature of the fire in the warehouse must have reached 1525 degrees Centigrade (2775 degrees Fahrenheit) to have melted the head of the column.

Molten cast-iron column, from the London Docks, 1940

George Walker

Photograph of George Walker with his George Medal, awarded in 1941

The war years saw many individual acts of bravery by men, women and children. On the 7 September 1940, the Royal Albert Dock suffered extensive damage from heavy bombing. Two PLA constables, Edward George Walker and John Henry Newton, transported casualties to hospital. They also boarded a burning vessel, under fire, to rescue other casualties. Both men were awarded the George Medal in recognition of their bravery. In May 1941, the *PLA Magazine* noted that they had 'displayed courage and devotion to duty on many occasions.' On 22 July 1941, Mrs Winston Churchill awarded George Medals to both men, and to twenty other PLA employees.

Wartime voices

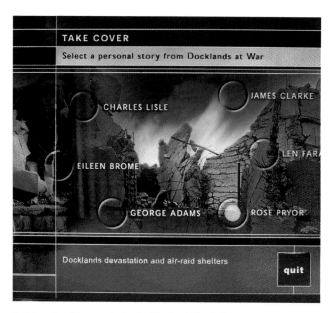

An interactive AV screen in the Docklands at War Gallery

Five interactive screens make interesting use of selected wartime memories. Eileen Broome, a typist at the West India Docks, describes the events of 7 and 8 September 1940:

'To most of us it was a sense of relief that it was the docks and not us, of course... the devastation was absolutely dreadful... ghastly... It was all burning and everything reduced to rubble... the clerks, the dockers, everybody, the bosses, they all went in and helped get all this mess cleared up... but they continued somehow to operate those docks.'

Molly Patterson

The River Emergency Service (RES) came into being in 1939 as a river-based Civil Defence Unit. The RES was responsible for rescue and ambulance duties and maintaining communications. Some 1500 volunteers operated a fleet of 170 small craft and fourteen ambulance vessels. Molly and Alexander Patterson joined the RES, and Molly became head of the medical stores at Brunswick Wharf, Blackwall. Some RES personnel did anti-invasion training exercises. Molly was issued with sealed orders, to be opened only in the event of an invasion.

RES membership certificate, whistle and recreational chessmen used by Molly Patterson, pictured in the white tunic

Siemens' Field Telephone

Siemens field telephone set, around 1940

Most London factories and workshops turned their production to supporting the war effort. With many men joining the armed forces, more women were recruited into manufacturing jobs. This military version of a portable magnetic field telephone was made at Siemens Brothers' electrical engineering and cable factory, Woolwich, around 1940. Sets like these were designed for use by the military and ARP divisions. Magnetic telephones were self-contained units, with handsets and ringing mechanisms, powered by batteries. In action, two phones could be readily wired up together, without a central operator.

Siemens Brothers' works – originally German owned – had a remarkable war record. Amongst its many challenges was managing production with a workforce reduced from 10,000 to 7000. The 14.2 hectares (35 acre) riverside site was one of the most intensively bombed in the country. Over 32,515 square metres (350,000 square feet) of factory floor space was destroyed. Siemens' cable ship, the *Faraday*, was wrecked in the Channel, by bombing in 1941. Despite this, the factory developed and produced military telephones and cables, and radar equipment in enormous quantities. The length of cable produced would

have gone around the world eighty times.

In April 1942, Siemens produced the first experimental section of the HAIS type PLUTO (Pipe Line Under the Ocean). Following further development and sea trials of this flexible armoured petroleum pipeline, Siemens began production in September 1943. Over 320 kilometres (200 miles) of the pipeline was produced, supplying vital fuel to the Allied troops in Normandy and Calais, and then overland into Europe. Throughout the war, Siemens maintained its own extensive Home Guard, ARP and firefighting units at the works.

Live Architecture

Not all Festival of Britain attractions were confined to the Southbank. An exhibition of architecture, town planning and building research was staged in Poplar, East London. The area had suffered immense damage during World War Two. The Live Architecture exhibition showcased the rebuilding of Poplar to 86,000 visitors.

Festival organisers were searching for a showcase of post-war rebuilding policies in action. Frederick Gibberd, festival adviser and eventual architect of Harlow New Town, suggested using a building project currently underway. Organisers settled on the part-completed Lansbury Estate in East London for what became the exhibition of 'Live Architecture'.

The Lansbury project illustrated construction of a 'model' community. Layout was influenced by the principles of the County of London Plan. Space, light and population density were primary concerns. Schools, churches and social amenities were central to its infrastructure.

Lansbury proved an ideal setting for the 'Live Architecture' exhibition. The route through the new estate took visitors past displays on problems symptomatic of previous house building. Rising damp, smoky rooms and structural faults were compared with new preventative techniques.

Proposed patio
in The Architect
After a sketch b

ew homes
se from
ondon's
ins . . .

PLAR

Alice Snoddy and family with pet tortoise Topsey, are handed the keys to their new home on the Lansbury Estate by Reginald Stamp (Chairman of London County Council Housing Committee).

Boxes reproduced clothing from Southbank to the Live Architecture exhibition at Lansbury. Some included Dan-Air style, borrowed from Scandinavian fashion.

New Port, New City
Post-1945

Nothing could have prepared local communities for the scale and pace of economic and social change which swept through London's post-war port area. Successfully rebuilt by 1955, much of Docklands was in a state of decline and dereliction by 1975. Plans to regenerate Docklands were hotly contested and its eventual rebirth was hard-won.

The opening of new container berths at Tilbury, in 1968, sealed the fate of the old up-river docks. Closures began in 1967, and in 1981 even the once mighty Royal Docks group had closed. Wharf, factory and business closures followed. Despite plentiful earlier plans, the reshaping of Docklands only began with the creation of the London Docklands Development Corporation (LDDC) in 1981. Under government direction, the LDDC was charged with the physical, economic and social regeneration of 22 square kilometres (8.5 square miles) of inner London. Docklands' groups fought hard to establish a 'fair deal' for local residents, both campaigning against, and working with the LDDC and developers.

Since 1981, new transport networks, new housing, new businesses and new leisure space have transformed Docklands. Canary Wharf, with its landmark towers, is now London's second business district. Multinational companies now work where ocean-going ships once tied up. The area's multicultural residential mix reflects both its trading past and its trading present. Fittingly, the Port of London remains the country's largest port, although its main activities are now located down river.

The gallery display about the Lansbury Estate, Poplar, in 1951

Royal Albert Dock

This photograph of the Royal Albert Dock was taken in 1964. The busy scene of cranes, ships and lighters gives no indication of the cargo handling revolution, which would shortly transform the Port of London. Containerisation received a major boost with the standardisation of container dimensions in 1965. The Port of London Authority invested heavily in seven new container berths at Tilbury Docks, opened in 1968. Unsuited to the handling of large container shlps, the closure of the upriver docks began in 1967. The Royal Docks closed in 1981.

Photograph of the Royal Albert Dock, 1964

Sailors' Society sign

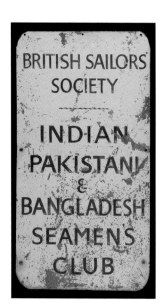

Sailors' Society sign, around 1971

This painted sign was removed from the British Sailors' Society building, at Tilbury Docks. The sign dates to around 1971, after the separation of Bangladesh from Pakistan. Seamen from the Indian sub-continent had been known as Lascars, originally working on East India Company ships in the eighteenth century. Lascars were mostly Muslim seamen from Calcutta, Bombay, Chittagong and Sylhet. Highly regarded by British ship-owners, Lascars earned only a fifth of British sailors' wages in the 1930s. During the war one third of British merchant seamen was Asian. Over 6000 Indian merchant sailors were killed by enemy action. The pay and conditions of Asian seamen improved dramatically during the war, mostly due to the action of Aftab Ali's Indian Seamen's Union, based in Calcutta. Today's thriving Bengali community in Tower Hamlets originates from the settlement of Lascar sailors in the 1930s.

The Beatles

Photograph of the Beatles at Wapping, 1968 (Courtesy Tom Murray)

Tom Murray took this photograph of the Beatles at Wapping in July 1968. The group was taking a break from recording what would later be known as the *White Album*. Fed up with relentless media attention, the Beatles decided to have one last day of 'mad photographs.' Don McCullin was contracted for the photo shoot and hired a *Sunday Times* freelance photographer, Tom Murray, to assist. McCullin shot in black and white, while Murray worked in colour. Five London sites were selected for the sessions, including the area around Wapping Pierhead. The group was photographed on the pierhead and on the river beach. The day after, the Beatles started work on their next single, *Hey Jude*, at Abbey Road Studios.

Wapping Pierhead was part of the original Wapping Entrance to the London Docks. This entrance ceased to be used in 1957. The London Docks closed to shipping in October 1968. The period 1968 to 1972 also saw the closure of St Katharine Docks, the Surrey Commercial Docks and many riverside wharves. Between these closures and later regeneration, Docklands was extensively used as a location for photographic shoots, television drama programmes and films.

No Locks on the Docks poster

The first phase of up-river dock closures culminated in the shutting of the Surrey Commercial Docks in 1970. Between September 1967 and January 1970, thirty-two riverside wharves ceased trading. Many Docklands factories closed during the same period. The impact of these closures on the local residential and business communities was immense. Around 150,000 jobs were lost in the five Docklands boroughs between 1966 and 1976. Many of these losses were directly attributable to the closure of the docks. The 1970s saw numerous frustrated proposals for the regeneration of Docklands. Represented on the Docklands Joint Committee, the Docklands Forum acted as the main channel of expression for local community and interest groups. One of the main community objectives was the protection of traditional port employment. The late 1970s was a time of severe financial crisis for the Port of London Authority (PLA). As a result, the PLA made various proposals for the closures of the West India and Millwall Docks, and the Royal Docks, between 1976 and 1978.

The PLA's announcements brought immediate opposition. The Docklands Forum waged the successful *No Locks on the Docks* campaign throughout 1976, to retain the West India and Millwall Docks. This striking poster was

No Locks on the Docks poster, 1976

produced for the Bethnal Green and Stepney Trades Council. It was printed by Anvil Printers, a trade union printing house. The poster used a simple but extremely effective graphic style to convey a powerful message. In May 1978, the PLA announced the closure of both upper docks. After intense political activity, however, they

received a short-term reprieve, and the PLA examined various schemes for rationalising cargo operations there. Unfortunately, the conventional cargo tonnages handled at both docks continued to decline. Further losses resulted in the closure of the West India and Millwall Docks in 1980, and the Royal Docks in 1981.

'Fortress Wapping' mug

'Fortress Wapping' mug, 1986

In 1986, print workers at News International went on strike and picketed the new printing plant at Wapping. With the move away from Fleet Street to the old London Docks site, News International attempted to introduce new working practices. Faced with opposition from the print unions, members of the electricians' union were employed to operate the new printing machinery. The streets of Wapping became the focus of pickets, marches and demonstrations. The strike collapsed in 1987, without the reinstatement of sacked workers. This mug was one of the many souvenirs produced in support of the strikers.

Docklands Light Railway

When the London Docklands Development Corporation came into being in 1981, one of its immediate tasks was to improve the area's infrastructure. By 1983, over eighty infrastructure projects were under way. These included road building, new sewer pipes, improved gas and electric mains, fibre-optic networks and land reclamation.

Docklands Light Railway train card, 1991

In 1984, the Docklands Light Railway was commissioned to link the Isle of Dogs with Tower Hill in the west and Stratford in the east. The original budget for the DLR was £77 million. Contracts to lengthen station platforms and for double-length trains were let in 1987. This tube card promoted the DLR link to Bank underground station, which opened in July 1991.

In 1994 the DLR eastern extension to Beckton was opened. A southern extension to Greenwich and Lewisham was opened in 2000. The DLR has been vital to Docklands' regeneration.

Community poster

Poster designed by the Docklands Community Project for the Cherry Garden Action Committee, Bermondsey, around 1985

During the 1980s there was a dramatic level of campaigning activity from a wide range of community action groups in Docklands. Well-focused and publicised protests were directed at the London Docklands Development Corporation (LDDC) and property developers. Both were seen as disregarding the needs of local communities. The Docklands Community Poster Project designed this poster for the Cherry Garden Action Committee, Bermondsey.

Led by artists Lorraine Leeson and Peter Dunn, the Docklands Community Poster Project was created in 1980. Funded by the Greater London Council (GLC), the project aimed at creating a powerful artistic realisation of community views and aspirations as Docklands began regeneration. The artists worked co-operatively with community action groups, developing poster designs to present their concerns. Artwork was also produced for leaflets, pamphlets, exhibitions, demonstrations and river processions, including the People's Plan Armadas to Parliament (1984–1986).

The Docklands Community Poster Project acquired eight billboard sites to display eighteen very large posters. Cut-and-paste photomontage techniques were cleverly used to create billboard posters with direct and often humorous comments on regeneration. Adding new material to the posters created a 'series' effect. The community messages could then be unfolded in instalments, with each new version of the posters. Placed in prominent public locations, the billboard posters highlighted housing, health, employment and transport concerns.

In 1990, the Docklands Community Poster Project became refocused as the 'Art of Change' with a growing emphasis on issues of multicultural identity and values.

Towering Ambition

This powerful charcoal drawing, by Fay Ross-Magenty, presents an artist's view of part of the second phase of development at Canary Wharf. The viewer's eye is taken upwards to the strong verticality of the buildings, echoed by the construction cranes. The new Citibank tower at 25 Canada Square, designed by Cesar Pelli, appears on the right. Out of view is the HSBC tower at 8 Canada Square, designed by Foster and Partners. The pair of forty-two-storey skyscrapers were built between 1997 and 2003. At the centre of the drawing is Cesar Pelli's Canary Wharf Tower, at 1 Canada Square, completed in 1992. By 2003, Canary Wharf provided jobs for around 100,000 people.

Towering Ambition,
by Fay Ross-Magenty, 2001
(Courtesy of the artist)

Lustreware dish

In March 1992 the Government formally approved a sixteen kilometre (ten mile) extension of the Jubilee Line to Docklands. The route was to be from Green Park, via Waterloo and London Bridge, to Canary Wharf and Stratford. Construction occupied the period 1993 to 1998. The Museum of London Archaeological Service created a major programme of excavations. The London Bridge area revealed important Roman and post-medieval finds. This early seventeenth-century copper lustreware dish depicts the head of a turbaned man, and was probably imported from Catalonia, in north-eastern Spain.

Spanish lustreware dish

Mudlarks Gallery

The Mudlarks Gallery is an interactive space for children under eleven. It is a fun learning area, where children can explore a variety of activities.

Welcome Zone
- Meet the cartoon characters, Elli Phant and Stevie Dore, who will act as guides
- Sniff the 'smelly pipes'

Early Years Zone
- Enjoy the soft play area, with its climbing frames, chute and Docklands Light Railway Train
- Put together the Docklands' giant jigsaw

Map Zone
- Discover a range of commodities and where they came from

Building Zone
- Construct some of Docklands' landmark buildings
- Touch and match the building finishes used at Canary Wharf

Dock Work Zone
- Meet some of the 'dock people' and the tools of their trades
- See how cargoes were weighed on a beamscale
- Use ropes and pulleys to make light work of lifting
- Balance a clipper ship with cargo

Waterworks Zone
- Tie some of the knots used on ships and in the docks
- Take a look inside the big diving helmets
- See what you can find hidden on the foreshore discovery beach
- Try and spot the real archaeological foreshore finds

Visitor Information

Opening hours

Seven days a week, 10.00am–6.00pm
(last admission 5.30pm)
Smoking, eating and drinking are not allowed
in the galleries. Photography is allowed only
in designated areas.
For recorded information: Tel 0870 444 3856

Shop

The Museum Shop stocks a wide range of gifts
and souvenirs about the docks and their history.
There is an extensive range of children's books
and specialist publications.
Enquiries and mail order: Tel 020 7001 9803
Email docklandsshop@museumindocklands.org.uk

Coffee Stop

Open seven days a week, 10.00am–5.30pm, the
Coffee Stop offers drinks, sandwiches, cakes and
snacks.

1802 Bar, Lounge and Dining

This new eating and drinking emporium combines
comfortable sofas and cool seating with industrial
décor. Lunch on the best of British bistro food, or
choose from a range of exotic cocktails at the
bar. Open Mon–Fri, 11.00am–11.00pm, Sat 12.00
noon–11.00pm, Sun 12.00 noon–5.00pm.
For bookings: Tel 0870 444 3866

Disabled access and facilities

The Museum in Docklands is fully accessible to
wheelchair users. Wheelchairs and powered
scooters can be borrowed free of charge. Audio
tours are available at the admission desk. Guide
and assistance dogs are welcome.
For further information about access:
Tel 0870 444 3855

Education and Events

The Museum in Docklands offers a full
programme of events for families and adults,
including workshops, demonstrations and study
days. Services for schools and colleges include
object handling, storytelling, evening classes and
teachers' courses and resources. For full details
of current programmes: Tel 020 7001 9814

Group visits

Pre-booked school and college parties are free
of charge. Adult groups of ten or more, booking
in advance, are entitled to a 20 percent discount.
For bookings: Tel 0870 444 3855

Picture Library

The Museum of London Picture Library holds over
35,000 images, illustrating the history of London
and its people, including Docklands.
To request a search or to order transparencies,
prints or slides: Tel 020 7814 5605
Email picturelib@museumoflondon.org.uk
Digital images from the collection can be
ordered from www.heritage-images.com

Filming

The Museum building and galleries provide
a unique location for filming.
For details of conditions and fees:
Tel 020 7814 5605
Email picturelib@museumoflondon.org.uk

Private and commercial hire

The Museum can be hired for a range of events
during the day and evening. The galleries offer
a vibrant contemporary space for evening
receptions of up to 800 guests – plus dining
for up to 50 people – while the stunning Chris
Ellmers Gallery can host up to 160 for dining
and many other kinds of functions.
For conferences and seminars, there is a 145
seat purpose-built Lecture Theatre with an
adjoining break room. There is also a small
Boardroom, seating up to 16 delegates, with
views over the quayside.
For further information: Tel 020 7001 9816
Email specialevents@museumindocklands.org.uk

Supporting the Museum in Docklands

For information on how to become a Friend of the
Museum in Docklands or become involved in the
Museum's development programme as a
corporate partner or sponsor:
Tel 020 7814 5507